365

Things to Do Before You Go to HEAVEN

D0048234

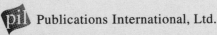 Publications International, Ltd.

Contributing Writers: Christine Dallman, Deana Deck, Lydia Harbert, Carol Stigger

Cover Photos: PhotoDisc Collection

Louis Weber, CEO
Publications International, Ltd.
7373 North Cicero Avenue
Lincolnwood, Illinois 60712

ISBN-13: 978-1-4127-0291-1
ISBN-10: 1-4127-0291-7

Manufactured in U.S.A.

8 7 6 5 4 3 2 1

The Long and Winding Road to Heaven

You found this book—or this book found you—because God gave you a unique purpose in life, and God gives you dreams. You can find that purpose, and you can make some dreams come true by remembering each day to live life to the fullest and celebrate the joys that come your way.

To some, that just comes naturally, but others need a little more encouragement. We've simplified the process by offering one suggestion per day to help you become a better person, learn something new about yourself, accomplish a goal, or realize a dream.

Allow yourself a few minutes every day to consider the day's suggestion, and ponder how you can personalize it to fit your life and your unique talents and interests. Some suggestions may not be right for you, but they may lead you to discover something else that you've always wanted to do. Perhaps you can't climb Mount Everest, but you can climb that mental mountain that's keeping you from making a phone call you've been putting off.

You are the gift you give to the world, and the world has gifts for you. Take a few minutes each day to open them. Who knows … the suggestion on a particular day may be the key to unraveling a hidden surprise. Or you may read a suggestion and realize it's not for you but perfect for someone you care about.

Realize that today is the first day of the rest of your life. You are a work in progress, and you have a lot to do and experience before you get to heaven. This book will encourage and inspire you to seize the day and live life to the fullest no matter who you are, where you live, or what your spiritual beliefs and practices may be. Embrace your individuality. Remember every day how special you are and that your Creator surrounds you with love and good things. *Carpe diem!*

☐ *1.* Make one realistic New Year's resolution and write it on the first day of every month of your calendar. Tell your best friend your resolution and promise to take him or her out to celebrate on December 1 if you keep your promise to yourself that long. This will give your friend a personal interest in giving you subtle reminders.

☐ *2.* Read the Bible from cover to cover in one year. Many study bibles include a schedule to guide your reading. Also, there are many devotional Web sites that offer schedules to keep you on track and allow you to select the order in which to read— straight through, historically, chronologically, or using a combined approach.

☐ *3.* Take a child ice-skating at Rockefeller Center in New York City. Wear matching mittens and scarves. Afterward, tell your young companion the story of *Hans Brinker and the Silver Skates* over cookies and a cup of hot chocolate. Then, go to the bookstore together and buy the child a copy of the book.

☐ *4.* Learn a new skill or take up a new hobby, even if you think you might not be good at it. You won't know unless you try. Who knows who you'll meet, who you'll make laugh, and who you'll surprise while pursuing your new activity.

☐ **5.** Shovel snow from an elderly
neighbor's sidewalk while singing an upbeat,
seasonal song and wearing a colorful scarf.
Don't forget to spread deicing salt and
return with your shovel when snow falls
again. You may get cold, but knowing you
did something kind for someone in need
will warm your heart and theirs.

☐ **6.** Build a snowman, and don't forget
to add a carrot for the nose. Use other
household items for eyes and a mouth.
Invite your neighbors to help build a snow
family and an igloo as well. Send photos to
everyone you know living or vacationing in
a warm climate.

☐ **7.** Break a bad habit or an addiction before it breaks you. Choose to do without it just for today. If you can extend the time beyond today, go for it! Otherwise, consider how you might get support in kicking the habit. Remember that God is with you cheering you on and helping you every step of the way.

☐ **8.** Write a personal mission statement with rules to live your life by. Follow your rules for a week, then review them and make revisions if needed. Try to reevaluate your rules every week. Be on the lookout for opportunities that bring your life closer in line with the life you envisioned when you wrote your mission statement.

☐ **9.** Learn greetings in a variety of languages, just in case the first person you meet in heaven speaks a different language. "Hello" is the obvious greeting, but you can be prepared to say more. For example: "Isn't it beautiful here?" or "Happy to see we both made it."

☐ **10.** Get in shape! Remember your body is a temple of the Holy Spirit, so take good care of it. It needs fruits and vegetables, brisk walks, bending and stretching, and a positive attitude. Learn to love the parts you do not like and cannot change by remembering that God made you and loves you just the way you are.

☐ *11.* When someone is having a bad day, listen. Turn off the TV and cell phone. Give them your full attention as well as a comfortable chair, a handkerchief if needed, and comfort food, such as a cookie. Don't offer advice, but give them a compliment before they leave. That night, say a short prayer for them and thank God for choosing you to be someone's angel today.

☐ *12.* Go sledding. If you don't have a sled, use a large piece of cardboard. Challenge people to race uphill with you. Invite other sledders to join you in a snowball-throwing contest. See how many activities you can organize for your own snow Olympics for children of all ages.

☐ *13.* Visit the travel section of a bookstore or library and recall which states or countries most intrigued you as a child or interest you now. Imagine how you would get there: car, train, boat, bus, plane, or motorcycle. Decide who you would go with or if you would rather go by yourself.

☐ *14.* Visit or call a travel agent to find out how much a trip to your dream destination would cost by every mode of transportation you would enjoy. Tell the agent that this is your dream trip and discuss your budget. Pick up brochures about your destination and keep them in a special folder. Stick a brochure on your refrigerator or bulletin board.

☐ *15.* Decide if your dream trip is possible—even if it's ten years from now— and figure out how much you'll need to save every week or month to take the trip. Then, start saving. Put these savings in a special account. You'll be surprised at the corners you're willing to cut for your dream trip.

☐ *16.* Talk to God. He's always listening. He won't yawn, interrupt you, turn on the TV, think you talk too much, or criticize your thoughts, opinions, or tone of voice. Tell him everything that is on your mind, even if you think it is trivial. Don't stop talking until you are ready to do so. Then, remain silent for a few minutes because God may have something to say to you.

☐ *17.* Write down your family history,
stories, and recipes for future generations.
Put them in a special scrapbook with photos
and newspaper clippings. Be sure to add
your name and the date. You'll enjoy writing
it as much as people will enjoy reading it
decades from now.

☐ *18.* Buy some food (such as a sand-
wich and a drink) for a homeless person
standing on the street corner holding a sign.
You may be an answered prayer, saving
someone from utter despair. You may even
renew a desperate person's faith. At the very
least, you'll feel that you responded to an
ocean of need by not looking away and by
making a difference in your own way.

☐ **19.** Write an unexpected letter to a friend (not an e-mail). In this technological age, handwritten letters are becoming much more rare, but they have a more personal touch. Writing a letter shows that you think your friend is worth the extra time and a postage stamp. A personal letter can mean so much more than an e-mail—and what a treat to find a real letter in the mailbox along with bills and junk mail.

☐ **20.** Put together a jigsaw puzzle with a child. Let the child pick out the puzzle, and ask him or her questions about the scene. Enter the child's world with interest and enthusiasm. You'll learn more about your young friend just by listening.

☐ *21.* Grow your hair long, then donate it to Locks of Love, an organization that makes hairpieces for people suffering from medical hair loss. To find out more, visit www.locksoflove.org. Share the news about this organization and encourage friends to donate their hair as well. You could make it a family or club project.

☐ *22.* Treat your family to summer in January. Pack a picnic basket and spread a sheet on the living room floor. Turn up the heat, turn on all the lights, and tell your family to wear sunglasses, shorts, and sandals. Serve their favorite picnic foods. If you have a fireplace, you could even toast some marshmallows!

☐ *23.* Find your best friend from grammar school. This may not be as difficult as you think. Ask other classmates, especially the person who organizes your reunions. Or try searching for your friend on the Internet at www.classmates.com or www.reunion.com. You never know, he or she might be looking for you, too!

☐ *24.* Make a list of all the books that you've been wanting to read. Prioritize them and schedule a block of time each day for reading. You might want to create a reading nook with a good lamp, a comfortable chair, and a coaster for your favorite beverage. Be a consistent page turner. If you go on a trip, take the book with you.

☐ **25.** Try a new food. Next time you're at your favorite restaurant, order something you haven't tried before. You might be disappointed in the texture or taste, but you won't regret the feeling of freedom that comes from breaking your routine. If you like it, try similar foods the next time or find out how to prepare them at home.

☐ **26.** Sign the back of your driver's license or organ donor card, and inform your family members so they are aware of your wishes. Visit www.shareyourlife.org for more information about the lives that have been saved thanks to organ donors and what a miracle it is to pass on the gift of life.

□ **27.** Volunteer your time at a:
- food bank
- home for the physically or developmentally challenged
- homeless shelter
- hospital
- nursing home
- orphanage
- pet shelter
- prison ministry
- soup kitchen
- veteran's home
- women's shelter

Then, find out what items the organization needs, such as toiletries, toys, books, and clothing. Enlist the help of friends to fill a bag with these items.

☐ **28.** Visit a concentration camp or read a book by a camp survivor. Vow to never let an atrocity such as the Holocaust happen again. Help stem the tide of hate by educating children and young people about what happens when hate clutches entire countries. It is a difficult lesson to teach and hard for people to hear, but without knowledge, history repeats itself.

☐ **29.** Invite friends to attend church with you. Then, invite them to join you for brunch afterward. They may wish to discuss their experience and learn about yours. If not, simply sharing the blessing of food is a quiet testimony to God's goodness.

☐ **30.** Organize a card shower for someone who is hospitalized, homebound, or having a special birthday. Notify "guests" by phone, mail, e-mail, or in person. Be sure to detail the reason for the shower and the guest of honor's address. Tell shower participants to send real cards, not e-mails. Follow up with a report on the results and a thank-you to all participants.

☐ **31.** Take a cruise to Alaska, the Caribbean, the Greek Isles, or another exotic destination with your best friend or several good friends. If you can't decide where to cruise, play "pin the ship on the globe"—the grown-up version of pin the tail on the donkey—and take a cruise there.

☐ *32.* On a cold day, purchase a dozen donuts or bagels and cups of coffee and hot chocolate. With a friend, drive around delivering the goodies to homeless people you see on the street. It will do more than warm them physically; it will also warm their hearts to know that somebody cares.

☐ *33.* Teach someone to read. It sounds rather daunting, but you can do it with the help of the book *You Can Teach Someone to Read* by Lorraine Peoples. Contact your library to find an illiterate person who is waiting for someone like you to open the doors to the written word and the magic of books.

☐ *34.* Create a family tree or research your ancestors. Tracing your family history can be frustrating, challenging, and time-consuming. But it's also rewarding to learn about your ancestors—where they came from, what they did, where they lived, and their hopes and dreams. How deeply can you dig into your family roots? Talking to older relatives can help you get started, as can genealogy Web sites.

☐ *35.* Make a snow angel if your winter weather allows. If not, make a sand angel to watch over all the sand castles. Sand is harder to dust off your clothing, but if the sun is warm and the water is cool you'll be willing to pay the price!

☐ **36.** Forgive someone: parents, children, friends, yourself. If necessary, several times a day, say to yourself, "I forgive _____," and eventually, you will. Wipe the slate clean and open the door to love that person again, or walk away with peace of mind. Remember that holding a grudge against someone allows that person to live in your head rent-free.

☐ **37.** Give a massage to a friend or loved one. But first find out how to perform a few simple, but professional maneuvers. When done properly, a massage can relax a person, relieve tension, and make them feel pampered. Light some candles and use scented oils to add a special touch.

☐ *38.* Send Valentine cards to your
family members and friends, even to those
who are sometimes difficult to love—
especially those who are difficult to love.
Save the most beautiful card for the most
challenging person on your list. That is the
person whose day needs sweetening the
most. Yours may be the only Valentine card
he or she receives.

☐ *39.* Memorize a few of your favorite
quotes and then drop them into conversa-
tions when appropriate. The well-known
phrase of 14th century mystic Julian of
Norwich, "All shall be well, and all shall be
well, and all manner of things shall be well,"
applies to most of life's moments.

☐ **40.** Ask someone standing on the sideline to dance. If someone is unable to dance, sit down and talk with them. Introduce your new buddy to your friends and include him or her in your evening. You might just make an interesting new friend.

☐ **41.** Practice meditation, which can be simply sitting back, relaxing, and emptying your mind of every care, concern, and to-do list. Just enjoy being in the moment and being in the place where you are. Notice the sounds and the scents. Feel the air on your face, feel the cares slipping out of your mind and onto the floor. You can pick them up later. Even God took a day off after creating the world. You can, too!

☐ *42.* Practice the art of handholding. Seize every opportunity to hold someone's hand: a friend's hand while walking down the street, a loved one's hand while watching a sunset or a movie, a child's hand on the way to bed, and your own hand when you need comfort, courage, or a moment to reflect on what's going on around you.

☐ *43.* Say "I love you" to all your loved ones. Speak it, whisper it, write it, e-mail it, phone it, sing it, rhyme it, say it with flowers, say it with brownies, say it with hugs, feel it in your heart, and mean it when you say it. Don't be surprised at the love you receive in return!

☐ *44.* Send a poem that expresses your feelings to someone you care about. *Sonnets from the Portuguese* by Elizabeth Barrett Browning is a good place to start. Shakespeare's sonnets contain a gold mine of feelings. If you've saved them, last year's Valentine cards may contain the perfect poem. Or, you can write your own.

☐ *45.* Visit a greenhouse or conservatory. During the bleak months of winter, spending a day surrounded by exotic plants, colorful flowers, and warm floral-scented air is a surefire way to beat the winter blues. It will remind you that spring is on its way. Start planning the flowers you will plant in your yard or window box this spring.

☐ **46.** Write down the last name of everyone you love. Find out in which country the name originated. Learn to write "I love you" in each country's language. Then, write a letter or e-mail to all your loved ones telling them you love them in their special language. There are several online services that provide translations from English to many major languages.

☐ **47.** Try to love everyone you meet today unconditionally. Do not judge their faults, the wrongful things they've done or said, the mistakes they've made, or the way they're living their lives. See them as God does—people with flaws yet deserving of all the love you can give them.

☐ **48.** The fruits of God's spirit are joy, love, peace, patience, kindness, generosity, faithfulness, gentleness, and self-control. Pick one fruit you'd like to see grow in your life. Ask God to help you. Then, identify that spiritual fruit with your favorite real fruit. Eat a serving each day as a tangible reminder of the spiritual fruit you are growing within your heart.

☐ **49.** Ladies—invite your girlfriends over for a pajama party. Watch chick flicks, eat popcorn, do each other's hair and nails, pass around women's magazines, and discuss the latest fashions. Gents—have the guys over for a friendly game of cards, and don't forget the chips and dip.

☐ **50.** Be thankful for the smile of a stranger. Remember the person did not have to acknowledge you, but some people just naturally make others feel welcome and good about themselves. Take a lesson from them and begin to smile at strangers whenever you feel it is safe to do so.

☐ **51.** Sponsor a child in a foreign country. For less than a dollar a day, you can support a needy child overseas through a reputable organization, such as World Vision, Save the Children, or Compassion International. Not only will you provide them with nutritious food, clean water, and medical care, you'll also be helping them gain an education and hope for the future.

☐ **52.** Be thankful for your child's laughter and encourage it every chance you get. A child has a right to be silly and to find you silly, the dog silly, and even great aunts silly. Let laughter rule your household. If you have a day with too little laughter, stop what you're doing and spend a moment with your child.

☐ **53.** Help sponsor an Olympic athlete (or Special Olympics athlete), and be part of a tradition that goes back more than 2,000 years and brings together people of several nations. The world has always celebrated and encouraged its athletes, but the tradition needs sponsors like you to keep the Olympic torch burning.

☐ **54.** Count your blessings. Start a blessings diary. Every night write down at least one good thing that happened since you woke up. You'll come to realize how much God truly loves you even on days that seem ordinary, boring, or difficult. On those days it is important to find a rose among the thorns.

☐ **55.** When the loved one of a friend passes on, make a personal visit and bring a gift, such as a bouquet of flowers or something to eat. Inviting a grieving person to "stop by anytime" isn't very appealing to someone who's struggling to get out of bed every day and to whom every minute feels like an hour.

☐ **56.** Write down an impossible dream, and think about ways you can make it come true. Set a deadline to have your dream accomplished, or create small goals and due dates to make your dream come true one step at a time. Then, go out and start making it happen! You can do it because somewhere deep inside, you always knew you could.

☐ **57.** Be kind to a stranger. You may be the only person to offer a smile and a helping hand today. An act of kindness can change a life or simply brighten a dreary day. And, that stranger just might be the person you have been waiting to meet or thought you would never meet.

☐ **58.** Visit three people in a nursing home or hospital. Ask the staff to recommend patients who do not get many visitors. Share God's love with lonely patients and remember that they may be afraid of their disease and limitations and worried about their future. Listen more than you talk. Find out their major concerns and promise to pray for their specific needs either during your visit or later, depending on their comfort level with prayer.

☐ **59.** Read a child a bedtime story. Choose a classic tale, such as *Peter Rabbit,* a chapter from *Charlotte's Web,* or a story that the child chooses. Be patient with the child's requests to reread favorite passages.

☐ *60.* Take a first-aid class, including CPR training. Keep your certification up-to-date and be willing to use your skills in an emergency situation before medical professionals arrive. Volunteer for school field trips and club outings that need a trained first-aid person. Who knows? You could save a life one day.

☐ *61.* Explore the ocean. Did you know that 80 percent of all living things live in the ocean? Take a closer look at what's going on down there. Whether you scuba dive, snorkel, submerge on a submarine, or visit an aquarium, you'll be amazed at the colors, sizes, shapes, and beauty of what you see.

☐ **62.** Mentor a child in a local program such as Big Brothers Big Sisters. You can be a role model and friend to a child who needs a positive influence in his or her life. You can be the one to help turn a child away from street gangs and drugs, help a child stay in school instead of dropping out, and give a child who cannot imagine being a success in life the confidence and determination to excel.

☐ **63.** Play a board game with children. Let them explain the rules and choose who gets to go first. If their rules differ from the printed ones, do not try to change the game. Ask questions even if you know the answers. Try to let one of the kids win.

☐ **64.** Organize your photos. Label them with names, dates, locations, and occasions. Add captions if you are so inspired. Put the photos into albums and share them with family members and friends. Mail the album with a few blank pages to out-of-town relatives and ask them to add a few photos. Be sure to include a return label and postage.

☐ **65.** Write a letter to a company whose product you like. In today's hectic world, people are much more likely to contact a company with a complaint. It will be a welcome surprise for them to receive a message of praise. You might even receive coupons for their products as a thank-you.

□ **66.** Return to your childhood home and ask for a tour. The new owners may not oblige, but if they do, remember a time when life was simpler, before you had a job and bills to pay and mouths to feed, when your future was a blank page waiting to be written. Don't the rooms look much smaller than they did when you were a kid?

□ **67.** Memorize a favorite Bible verse. Read the verse out loud five times a day, and you'll eventually commit it to memory. Be amazed at how it comes to mind when you least expect it or need it most. Then, memorize another verse, and soon you'll have your own mental Bible containing the verses that mean the most to you.

☐ **68.** Make a living will. A living will, or an advance health-care directive, is a legal document that informs family members of the course of treatment you would like to receive should you become incapacitated and unable to speak for yourself. Also, appoint a trusted family member or friend as your medical proxy who is authorized to make medical decisions that may not be covered in your living will.

☐ **69.** Learn the alphabet in American Sign Language so you can communicate with the deaf and translate if a deaf person is in trouble. Learn ASL online or take a class. By learning how to converse with deaf people, you'll enlarge your circle of friends.

☐ **70.** Have pie, ice cream, cookies, soda, or pizza for breakfast. Break your routine just this once. Do it on your birthday. Or surprise a family member on his or her birthday with a "favorite food" breakfast. Breakfast is said to be the most important meal of the day, so celebrate it.

☐ **71.** Volunteer your time with a cause that utilizes your special talents. Make a list of the things you can do, but be willing to take on simple tasks such as stuffing envelopes and making telephone calls. Every hour you give to a charity is worthwhile. Without your help, the organization would have to pay someone to do the work, leaving less money for its charitable services.

☐ **72.** Make matters better, not worse. When you hear a harsh word, respond with two kind ones. When you see an angry look, return it with a smile. When someone yells, whisper your response. When someone slams a door, open it and stand calmly in the doorway until they look back.

☐ **73.** Invite a friend to lunch for no particular reason. If he or she asks what the occasion is, say you do not need a reason to celebrate your friendship. Choose a restaurant you know your friend likes, even if it is not your favorite. And, no matter who may be on a diet, order two different desserts and share them. You can walk it off by window shopping or strolling through a park.

☐ **74.** Get your hair done just for fun. No reason necessary! See how many people notice. If nobody does, enjoy your little secret. A new hairstyle can be a perky pick-me-up any time of the week, and you do not need an excuse to pamper yourself occasionally. You are worth it!

☐ **75.** Throw an "unbirthday" surprise party on any date but the honored person's birthday. It will really be a surprise. Tell guests to bring cards for any occasion but a birthday. Use any holiday decorations except birthday ones. Serve a cake with lollipops on it, not candles. Have everyone make a wish for the guest of honor before you cut the cake.

☐ **76.** Kiss the Blarney Stone. Legend has it that this chunk of limestone will endow all who kiss it with eloquence and wit. The famous stone is part of the upper rampart of Lord Blarney's ancient castle, which dates back to 1446.

Blarney Castle and the Blarney Stone are located in southern Ireland, near Cork. Be sure to employ your new eloquence and wit with confidence.

☐ **77.** Give one of your treasures to a younger person and explain why it means so much to you. Or if you have something that you've been hanging on to but you don't use, give it to somebody you know would appreciate it and make good use of it.

□ **78.** Write a love note to your spouse or significant other. Hide it in a place where they'll find it when you're not around, such as a lunch bag, purse, gym bag, or suitcase. Or, hide it where they'll find it months from now. In the fall, you can put it with the spring gardening tools. In summer, you can slip it into a box of Christmas decorations.

□ **79.** Spring has sprung! Show you respect the environment and all of God's wonderful creations by cleaning up your corner of the world and maybe your neighbor's, too. As for the no-man's-land in the street and public parks, you can even clean up a little of that. Commit to filling one large bag with trash today.

☐ **80.** Write your life story. Everybody has a unique life story that no one else can tell. Whether you keep a daily journal, type up your autobiography, or record your story on a video or audio tape recorder, it will be a family heirloom. Who knows... it could become a best seller.

☐ **81.** Keep an extra $20 bill in your wallet, and tell God it is his money. The next time you see someone in need, ask God if he wants to help them. It may be a person in front of you at the grocery store who doesn't have enough money, or it may be someone whose wallet has just been stolen. God knows who the money is for, and, at the right time, so will you.

☐ *82.* Watch reruns of a program you loved as a kid. Invite someone close to your age to watch with you. Reminisce about how things were back then. Discuss what your dreams were and if they have come true or turned into other dreams. Remember the "good old days," and talk about what was really good and what could have been better.

☐ *83.* When you hear a siren, consider that shrill sound your call to prayer. Pray for the people in distress, as well as the firefighters, police officers, and paramedics who are rushing to help. Also, pray for bystanders that they may have the wisdom, courage, and strength to do what is necessary until the professionals arrive.

☐ **84.** If a friend or coworker is having a bad day or could use a lift, surprise him or her with a cupcake, a cup of soothing tea, or another goodie. Treat him or her to lunch. Find out his or her favorite color and leave a bag of jelly beans in that color on his or her desk the next morning.

☐ **85.** Ask for forgiveness from someone you've hurt. A personal visit is the most meaningful, and it allows for hugs. But if a visit is not possible, write a letter or send a card. Invite the person to respond but tell them that you understand if they do not. Maybe someday they will. At the very least, you have opened the door to reconciliation. Sometimes that is all we can do.

☐ **86.** It's time for spring-cleaning! De-clutter your house and your life. Make piles of items to sell, donate to charity, give to friends, keep, and throw away. You'll be amazed at how liberating it is to rid yourself of unwanted or unused items and how much space you free up in your drawers, closets, and garage. You'll probably find things you lost months ago and thought were gone forever.

☐ **87.** Visit an older relative that you haven't seen for a long time. He or she will appreciate your visit and any time you have to spend. Ask about family members who died before you were born and ask to hear stories about your relative's youth.

☐ **88.** Show children that Easter is about more than just the bunny. In addition to a basket, fill flowerpots with potting soil and packages of seeds, and include a small gardening tool with each pot. Help the child plant the seeds and set the pots in a window until it is time to plant them outside.

☐ **89.** When you see an elderly person or a parent with a baby struggling with packages, ask if you can help them to their car, into a taxi, or onto the bus. In this busy world, not many people are willing to take a few minutes to offer a little help that could make a big difference to someone whose burden is heavy.

☐ **90.** Visit all seven continents—Africa, Asia, Australia, Europe, North America, South America, and Antarctica. Leave something of your country and yourself on each continent: Make a small donation to a local charity, leave a map of your home state, or give a tour guide an American-made product.

☐ **91.** Take a magical mystery tour. Ride a city bus or commuter train to the end of the line. Explore the neighborhood. Have lunch at a local restaurant, window shop, stroll through parks, and talk to people. Bring home a souvenir, which could be something you purchased or even a fragrant wildflower or an interesting leaf.

☐ *92.* Feel free to make a fool of yourself today! Sing on a busy sidewalk. Ask someone you just met for a date. Wear silly socks. Greet people in a foreign language. Wear a goofy necklace or flowers in your hair. Take a chance and show the world it is fun to be foolish one day a year.

☐ *93.* Complete a century (100-mile) bicycle ride. Consult a personal trainer about getting in shape for this adventure, and plan your ride after the necessary training. Make sure your bike, as well as your body, can handle the journey. Plan your rest stops before you depart so you won't suffer from hunger or thirst in the middle of the wilderness.

☐ **94.** Learn to drive. It may be intimidating, or downright frightening, especially in a big city, but driving is a skill that enables you to visit places off the beaten path and not accessible by public transportation. Driving will make you feel liberated and independent, and it opens up a whole new world to explore.

☐ **95.** Slow dance. There's just something about holding the one you love in your arms and swaying to "your song." Dim the lights and let the rest of the world drift away. Don't talk. Just listen and feel. After the music ends, find a quiet corner and talk about your first dance and the first time you heard your special song.

☐ **96.** Plant a garden and grow your own produce. Growing your own food will give you a great sense of accomplishment. Share the fruits (and vegetables) of your labor with somebody who will enjoy them. Donate your extras to a homeless shelter or local food bank.

☐ **97.** Ride a cable car in San Francisco. The preferred mode of transportation for visitors to the City by the Bay, cable cars have been gliding down the streets of San Francisco since 1873.

Soak up the scenery, so when you're back home stuck in traffic, you can remember the beauty of San Francisco.

☐ **98.** Put money in somebody else's parking meter when it's expired . . . before they get a ticket! Think of other random acts of kindness you can accomplish. Make sure you don't leave home without some spare change jingling in your purse or pocket, reminding you that just a few coins can be enough to make someone's day.

☐ **99.** Be somebody's secret admirer. Let the person you choose know that he or she is special by saying nice things behind their back, sending unsigned cards, and leaving little treats on their porch or desk. Select someone who needs an ego boost. Too many good-hearted souls go through life unnoticed and unrewarded.

☐ **100.** Leave a nice handwritten note in a library book for the next reader to find. Tell them what parts you particularly enjoyed and if you have read any other books by that author. List a few other books you have enjoyed and wish the reader a nice day. Just don't reveal how the book ends!

☐ **101.** Attend the symphony and buy the best ticket you can afford. If your budget is lean, colleges and universities often have free concerts. Check your local newspaper for outdoor and community concerts, which are often free as well. Decide if you want to include season tickets in your budget next year or if once a year is enough for your spirit.

☐ ***102.*** Have a pillow fight and include everyone in the household. Use every pillow and every room in the house. Be sure to remove breakables before beginning the event. If you have a pet that scares easily, it may be better off outside. Have a camera handy and send photos to relatives. Post a photo in your office. Who says families don't have fun together anymore!

☐ ***103.*** Visit every state in the country, including Alaska and Hawaii —*especially* Alaska and Hawaii! Then, go to Puerto Rico to reward yourself. This can be a lifelong project, so start planning now. Requesting brochures from the cities and states on your route is easy to do online.

☐ **104.** Pay your taxes. Feel free to complain that tax forms are confusing and taxes are too high. Drive your tax return to the post office at the last minute and join the parade of fellow grumbling citizens. Then, sleep easy knowing that thanks to your taxes, the police and fire departments will respond if you call them and that Homeland Security is working 24/7.

☐ **105.** Travel by train. Watch the beautiful countryside roll by as you sit back and relax on your leisurely journey. It may take longer than traveling by air, but the rural scenery is spectacular and the urban scenery is an eye-opener. Mile after mile you get to stop traffic. Feel the power!

☐ *106.* Be a celebrity for a day. This could be as simple as getting your picture in the newspaper or as elaborate as dressing like a star (don't forget the dark sunglasses) and having a friend follow you around— carrying a walkie-talkie and acting as your bodyguard—while another friend follows you with a camera.

☐ *107.* Be a vegetarian for a week... or a month. Be sure to consult your doctor first, then do some research to help you in the process. Keep track of your weight and the money you spend on food. At the end of your vegetarian experience decide if not eating meat makes you feel healthier and/or saves you money.

☐ *108.* Donate blood. According to the National Blood Data Resource Center, an average of 38,000 units of blood are needed every day. To find out more, visit www.givelife.org or www.americasblood.org. Be sure to find out your blood type in case you ever need an emergency transfusion.

☐ *109.* Visit the Great Wall of China. This incredible monument began as many smaller walls built to protect against attacks. More than 2,000 years ago, Chinese emperor Qin Shi Huangdi linked these walls together. In all, it took more than 300,000 people to build the Great Wall, which measures some 4,000 miles—the distance from Chicago to Paris.

☐ ***110.*** Gather a group of friends to
sing songs at a retirement center or nursing
home—at a non-holiday time when residents get fewer visitors. Choose songs that
are familiar to most people, such as tunes
from old musicals or hymns, and invite
residents to sing along. Be sure to get
permission from the center ahead of time.

☐ ***111.*** Make a donation or contribution to a cause you believe in but haven't
actively supported; for instance, a nature
conservatory, an orphanage, an animal
shelter, a library, or the local firefighters.
Learn a little about the organization first to
make sure your contribution will be used
wisely and for the purpose you intended.

☐ *112.* Since 1970, Earth Day has been observed every April 22. Celebrate Earth Day by picking up litter in a park or along the side of the road. Remember that God gave humanity dominion over the earth, including the responsibility to care for it. Take a moment to thank God in advance for restoring the earth to its pristine state when he returns.

☐ *113.* Find something to smile about every day. This could be as simple as the sun shining, the blue sky, the birds chirping, the flowers blooming, a child smiling, a reflection in a puddle, or a colorful sunset. Praise God for the beauty of the world he created.

☐ *114.* Take in the view from atop the Sears Tower in Chicago. At 1,450 feet (1,729 feet with the TV antennae perched on top), the Sears Tower is the tallest building in the United States. From the Skydeck, you can see for 50 miles on a clear day, with four states visible. You can even feel the building gently sway on a windy day.

☐ *115.* Did you know that the last Friday of April is Arbor Day? Find a place in your yard, neighborhood, or local park to plant a tree and help it grow. If this seems like too much trouble, imagine being locked out of the house on a hot summer day with no shade trees in sight. For helpful tips, visit www.arborday.org.

☐ *116.* Schedule a day off from stress. Make a list of things that relax you— a drive, a walk, a good book or movie, a shopping trip, or a day spent fishing or gardening. Fill your day with activities you love. Let each restful moment fill your spirit and your soul. Can you do it again next week? Next month? Be sure that each month your calendar includes a day for *you.*

☐ *117.* Join a book club. Inquire at your local library or bookstore about book clubs in your area. Or hunt for a club online. Participate by reading the book all the way through before the meeting and thinking of questions and comments. Be ready to recommend a book if asked.

☐ ***118.*** Adopt or foster a pet from an animal shelter. According to the Humane Society of the United States, an estimated 3–4 million dogs and cats are euthanized in shelters every year. That's half of all dogs and cats entering the shelters each year. You can't save them all, but you can save one... or two... or three. And, of course, make sure to have your pet spayed or neutered.

☐ ***119.*** Send somebody flowers just because. Or, purchase a bouquet of flowers, leave them on someone's doorstep, knock or ring the doorbell, then run away. Hide where you can see the look of surprise on his or her face. It will warm your heart.

□ *120.* Skip down the block once in a while. Release your inner child and whistle a happy tune. View the world as if it were new to you. Listen to the birds, smell the flowers, and pick up treasures along the way, such as colorful leaves, stones, and wildflowers. Skipping releases stress, so you'll come home in a better mood.

□ *121.* Invent something. It doesn't have to be the world's greatest innovation, and you don't have to be Thomas Edison, but if you have an idea for a new product, why not try to make it a reality? Remember that the telephone and television were once just a dream, and computers and spaceships were merely science fiction at one time.

☐ *122.* Share your grandma's recipe with your best friend. But only if your grandmother didn't swear you to secrecy. If it's a secret family recipe that she entrusted you to keep, then keep it between the two of you ... until you're ready to pass it down to a daughter or cousin or niece who will keep the secret until it's time to pass it on to the next generation.

☐ *123.* Visit a farm or petting zoo in late spring or early summer. If you're not allergic to the animals, hold a baby bunny, let a kid goat nuzzle your hand, watch a foal and baby ducks follow their mothers, listen to the chirping of tiny chicks. Wonder at the miracle of new life.

☐ *124.* Be a contestant on a game show or a reality show. Find out where and how to apply and keep applying for as long as it takes. While waiting, be sure to watch the show you want to be on so you'll be the best contestant you can be.

☐ *125.* Face your fears. What do you fear the most? Are you afraid of heights? Enclosed spaces? Flying? Dying? Get in touch with what you fear and try to understand why you are afraid. It may be something in your past that you have forgotten or just part of your personality. Seek professional help if necessary, and remember God is always with you to protect you and give you courage.

□ *126.* Visit a country where you don't speak the language. Purchase a good guidebook and a foreign-language dictionary and do your best to communicate with the locals. They'll appreciate your effort and treat you with respect. You'll be proud of yourself for your ability to order a meal, buy a special souvenir, communicate with room service, and use local transportation.

□ *127.* Say "I love you" to somebody and show that you mean it. Do something they want to do even if you would rather do something else. Give them the TV remote. Have a conversation with the phone turned off. Prepare a meal of their favorite foods. Show them you care.

☐ *128.* Run or walk in a charity race.
If you're feeling extremely energetic, walk
60 miles in three days as you support the
fight against breast cancer. Take long walks
before the event to get in shape. Visit
www.the3day.org for more information.
You'll be healthier and you'll help cancer
patients in their fight to beat the disease.

☐ *129.* Get to really know your
parents, children, siblings, grandparents,
aunts, uncles, and cousins. For better or
worse, they are your family. Listen to their
stories and hear what they have to say. Once
you truly get to know them, you might be
surprised at how much you have in common
and how much you can learn from them.

☐ **130.** Visit the Taj Mahal. Located in Agra, India, the Taj Mahal was built by Emperor Shah Jahan as a mausoleum for his beloved wife. Constructed from about 1632 to 1650, this magnificent monument is made almost entirely from white marble. The most magical time to see it is under a full moon.

☐ **131.** Find someone to whom you can teach a skill. Schedule lessons if necessary, but keep it fun. Remember your favorite teacher and use his or her teaching style. Have a small party and graduation ceremony when your student masters the skill, and ask your student to pass on the gift of knowledge someday.

☐ *132.* Did you know that three billion people, nearly half of the world's population, live on less than two dollars a day? Many of them survive on meals of rice and beans. Eat only one cup of rice and one cup of beans for dinner and realize how fortunate you are. Then, donate the money that you saved on the meal to an organization such as Bread for the World, Heifer International, or the One Acre Fund.

☐ *133.* Live alone, even if only for a few months. It teaches you to take care of yourself and be independent. You will also learn to be your own best friend, comforting yourself when you're down and congratulating yourself on successful home repair jobs.

☐ *134.* Accept who you are and make peace with your body image. God makes people in all shapes and sizes, and he loves them no matter what. Maintain a healthy lifestyle by eating sensible portions of nutritious food and exercising regularly. Don't let bad habits ruin your health.

☐ *135.* Attend the prom or another formal gala. If you were unable to attend your high school prom, it's not too late. Sign up to be a chaperone at your local high school or attend a gala that requires formal attire. If you don't own the outfit you need, borrow it or rent it. Get your hair done and rent a fancy car or limousine if you can afford it.

☐ *136.* Stand up for your beliefs. Don't just say you support a cause . . . take an active role in it. Determine what causes you believe in, then research ways to get involved. You can make phone calls or speeches, design fliers or pass them out, and educate your friends. Remember that actions speak louder than words, and every cause needs enthusiastic, energetic activists.

☐ *137.* Plan to become financially independent. Make a list of your assets, debts, and anticipated expenses, then talk to your banker. A financial professional can advise you on how to achieve your goal, help estimate how long it will take, and detail the sacrifices you will need to make.

☐ *138.* Take someone who is confined to a wheelchair on a scenic drive or take them on a stroll, pushing their chair around the block or to a nearby park. Pack a picnic, find a lovely spot, and serve a leisurely lunch. Do not look at your watch or indicate that you need to be back at a certain time. Let this be a gift of time, not something you sandwiched between chores.

☐ *139.* Become one with nature for at least an hour today. Appreciate the warmth of the sun, the scent of the flowers, the shade of the trees, the melody of the birds. Really listen, see, smell, and feel what God reveals about himself through the world he created and renews every year.

☐ *140.* Give somebody an opportunity that you never had or a chance that you missed. Perhaps you didn't go to college, or due to age or health reasons you're no longer able to take your dream vacation. Instead of dwelling on what can no longer be, experience the joy that comes from selfless generosity.

☐ *141.* Ride a motorcycle. Drive if you dare, or ride behind an experienced driver. Enjoy the wind on your face, the feel of the road, the nearness of the neighborhood. Notice things you do not see from a car. Remember how much you're saving on gas. Don't forget to wear a helmet and hang on tight!

☐ *142.* Find something to laugh about every day—a funny thought, the playfulness of a dog, two squirrels frolicking in the yard, a TV commercial, a humorous greeting card, or a memory of a time you laughed so hard you couldn't stop. Laughter relieves stress, lightens the mood, and lifts the spirit. It really is the best medicine.

"Continual cheerfulness is a sign of wisdom."
—Irish proverb

☐ *143.* Beside the ocean, write a prayer for peace in the sand. Watch the tide come in and take your words out to sea. Imagine the waves delivering your prayer to beachcombers thousands of miles away.

☐ *144.* Take a ride in a glass-bottom
boat and view the mysterious underwater
world. Relish the rainbow of watery colors.
Notice the plants swaying with the currents.
See how many fish you can identify. Ask
about creatures you have never seen before.
Consider getting even closer by snorkeling
or learning to scuba dive.

☐ *145.* Take photos with family and
friends as often as possible. Relive the
memories when you need a laugh, a smile,
or just the comfort of home and family. Be
sure to label the photos with the date,
location, and occasion. Sadly, moments
that seem unforgettable now may be forgotten as the years pass.

☐ *146.* Arrive at the airport with your passport, credit card, ATM card, and a packed suitcase. Take the first flight available, wherever it is going. (If you need a visa, take the next plane.) While waiting to board, be sure to call your credit card company and your bank to tell them where you are going. If you don't, they may not approve your charges, and you might have even more adventure than you anticipated.

☐ *147.* Ride on a tire swing or tree swing. Laugh, smile, and enjoy the feeling of being a kid again as you twist, turn, and sway back and forth. If you can't find such a swing, install one in your yard or the yard of a neighbor who has children.

☐ **148.** Thank your teachers. Let them know they're appreciated. Whether you're a current student or facing your 25-year class reunion, a nice letter to let them know how they positively impacted your life would mean a lot to those who have dedicated their lives to educating others.

☐ **149.** Soar like a bird:
- go parasailing
- ride a zip line
- go hang gliding
- ride in a hot air balloon
- parachute out of an airplane
- ride a roller coaster

Or, simply lie down and remember the times you felt on top of the world.

☐ *150.* Dance! Take lessons to learn how to salsa, swing, polka, tap dance, waltz—whatever speaks to you the most. Just feel the beat and let your body sway to the music. Don't be afraid. And don't worry that other people may be watching. You're doing this for yourself.

Work like you don't need the money,
Love like you've never been hurt,
Dance like no one is watching.

—Irish toast

☐ *151.* Drive your dream car, even if only for a test drive. While driving, pretend you own the car. It's okay to feel on top of the world, even if only for a half hour.

□ *152.* Hold a butterfly in the palm
of your hand, being careful not to damage
its wings. Feel the whispery flutters and the
tiny pressure of its feet. Look at its eyes and
mouth and the iridescent scales on its
wings. View it as a work of art that you are
privileged to view. Then let it go and watch
it fly away until you can no longer see it.

□ *153.* Go cloud gazing with a child.
Look for shapes of things, such as animals,
and point them out to one another. The
child's buffalo may be your butterfly. Your
mashed potatoes may be the child's bowl of
ice cream. Talk about perspective and how
enriching it can be to see another person's
point of view.

☐ *154.* Celebrate summer with a picnic in the park, on the beach, or in your own backyard. Cook outside even if it's just hot dogs and marshmallows roasted on sticks over a small fire. Play outdoor games that the whole family can enjoy. Let the kids get as messy as they please. Wash them off in the lake, in a fountain, or with a garden hose. Giggles are guaranteed.

☐ *155.* Dance in the rain—alone, with a partner, or with a group. Let the sound of the wind and the patter of rain-drops be your music. Try a waltz, a polka, or see if you can dance like Gene Kelly in *Singin' in the Rain.* Stomp your feet in puddles to turn up the volume.

☐ *156.* *Carpe diem.* Seize the day. This day will not come again. Look for the magic moments and treasure them. They will not come to you again in the same way. As for bad moments, they will not return either, at least not in the same way. On average, a person has 28,105 days on Earth. Make each one count.

☐ *157.* Travel the Pacific Coast Highway. One of the most scenic highways in the country, this stretch of road will take you through Newport Beach, Los Angeles, Malibu, and San Francisco. You'll cross the Golden Gate Bridge and pass Hearst Castle as you witness some of the most breathtaking coastline in America.

☐ *158.* Serenade someone you care about on a clear night when the moon is full. Select a song that you know the person you're serenading likes. Even if you're not one of the Three Tenors, your effort will be appreciated. Remember: It's the thought that counts, not your ability to hit the high notes. When you're done, leave behind a single red rose.

☐ *159.* Take a horse-drawn carriage ride with a friend or loved one. If it's a daytime ride, bring an umbrella for shade and a container of lemonade. For a night ride, bring a small bouquet of flowers and some hot chocolate. Memorize a few lines of poetry to recite.

☐ *160.* Watch the sunrise and rejoice in the transition from night to day as the sun slowly moves over the eastern horizon. Appreciate the peace and tranquility of the early morning, listen to the birds chirping, and thank God for blessing you with the opportunity to greet the dawning of a new day. Check the weather section of your local newspaper for the projected sunrise time.

☐ *161.* Go kayaking. It's a great workout and a leisurely way to witness the beauty of nature and the wonderful world of the wilderness. See bears and moose from a safe distance. Listen to birds that fly closer to a silent craft. Dangle your hand in the water and just float for a while.

☐ *162.* Swim with dolphins. Many people report that the experience is mystical and that they feel a connection with the dolphins that join them to play in the water. Tropical vacation spots, such as Hawaii, Mexico, Florida, and California, offer visitors the opportunity to take a dive with these docile creatures.

☐ *163.* Ride in a convertible. Whether you own one or are just renting, there's nothing quite like the feel of the sun on your face and the wind in your hair as you drive along a scenic road with the top down. Get out of town. Head for the ocean, the mountains, or the woods. Just don't forget your sunglasses!

□ **164.** Listen more than you talk today. If someone asks why you're so quiet, tell them you want to hear what they have to say. Then, listen even harder while they talk. You may hear something important, something you need to know, something you never expected to hear, or just that you are an easy person to talk to.

□ **165.** Backpack through Europe. Traveling light and on a budget can sound like anything but a vacation to some, but exciting, intriguing, and spontaneous to others. With so much to do in so many countries, why not spend less and stay longer? There are numerous sites on the Internet to help you research your trip.

☐ *166.* On a night when the moon is just a crescent, take a blanket outdoors and lie on your back. See the new moon with the old moon in its arms. Then look for constellations. See if you can name them. Or, just count stars until you start to feel sleepy.

☐ *167.* Learn to change a flat tire. Check your car's manual for instructions. You never know when this valuable service could come in handy, either for yourself or an unfortunate stranger stranded on the highway. Do your children and yourself a favor and make them successfully change a tire in the driveway before their first solo driving experience. Otherwise, thanks to cell phones, they'll just call you for help.

☐ *168.* Teach someone how to drive.
Find an empty parking lot or a secluded
country road and give somebody the gifts of
freedom and independence. Get the "Rules
of the Road" for your state and help your
student study for the driver's exam. Go with
them to the exam, then take them out to
lunch to celebrate and to laugh over their
new driver's license photo.

☐ *169.* Sit on a park bench and tell
your life story, just like Forrest Gump. Talk
to pigeons, squirrels, insects, passersby,
dogs, and people who sit next to you. Don't
worry what they think of you. And if someone looks interested, it may be the beginning of a beautiful friendship.

☐ *170.* Find your happy place. If you love the outdoors, search forest preserves, beaches, and parks. If you enjoy reading, check out bookstores and libraries. If you like people-watching, try out every bench within walking distance. If you like to shop, treat yourself to a new item occasionally. Visit your happy place as often as possible.

☐ *171.* Do something special for somebody... anonymously. Pay for a stranger's coffee or meal; buy and deliver some groceries to a family in financial need; or leave a bouquet of flowers, homemade cookies, a friendly greeting card, or balloons on the doorstep of someone who lives alone or could use some cheering up.

□ *172.* String a hammock between two large shade trees and read a book while swaying gently until you fall asleep. Take a long nap. When you wake up, don't get up. Recall what you dreamed and think about what it might mean. Read more of your book. Try to stay in the hammock until it's too dark to read. You'll feel like you've been on vacation.

□ *173.* Live happily ever after. If you're married, work hard to stay together, even if it requires compromise and counseling. If you're not married, sign up with a reputable dating service or ask friends to fix you up. If you prefer being single, be the happiest single person in town.

☐ *174.* Climb a mountain. Or, if that's not feasible, hike to the top of the highest point in your region. Then breathe deeply and take in the view. Have someone take your photo and make that your Christmas card this year. Bring a small stone from the summit and place it on your desk to remind yourself that you can achieve great things.

☐ *175.* Treat your spouse or significant other as you did when you first met. Flirt, wear his or her favorite color, cook his or her favorite meal, look through photos of the two of you together, play your special song, and watch a movie you saw together when you first fell in love.

☐ *176.* Visit an elderly friend or relative and ask them to tell you a story about their childhood or another time. People from other generations have a different perspective on life because things were much simpler when they were younger. But some things never change, and you might be surprised at how similar your paths have been.

☐ *177.* Build a sand castle with a child. Remember that the child is the architect, not you. Half the fun is demolishing the castle, so join the demolition squad with enthusiasm—but first take a photo of the child with the sand castle. Give the child a copy of the photo.

☐ *178.* Make and bury or hide a time capsule with mementos and objects from the 21st century, such as a newspaper, magazine, instructions for operating the latest computer system, a few utility bills, and photos of the property where you are placing the time capsule. Enclose a letter describing a typical day in your life.

☐ *179.* Watch the sunset. See if you can spot a green flash. It's a flash of green light seen during the last few seconds of a sunset or sunrise. It's difficult to see a green flash because it happens so quickly, but it's best seen when the sky is free of clouds. Check the newspaper to determine your local sunset time.

☐ *180.* Go to an amusement park and ride every roller coaster. Ride your favorite one twice. Scream at the top of your lungs during every ride. It's a great way to release pent-up emotions. Then enjoy a snow cone and some cotton candy. You really can be a kid again.

☐ *181.* Pamper yourself. You deserve it! Get a facial, manicure, and pedicure. Get a massage, too. If it's out of your comfort zone, give yourself time to get used to the idea. Talk with others who enjoy massages. Relax and the tension will give way to comfort and peace. For an incredible experience, search for a place that gives Watsu massages in a pool of warm water.

☐ *182.* Take a road trip with your best friend. Pick a destination and decide what to do when you get there, but feel free to change your plans along the way. Pack hiking clothes, dressy clothes, and your swimsuit. Keep a trip diary. You'll both enjoy it for years to come.

☐ *183.* Learn to cook well. Take a class, pick up some cookbooks at a library or bookstore, exchange recipes with friends and family, and then start cooking! Discover your favorite home-cooked cuisine and begin to specialize. When you've mastered enough dishes for a complete meal, buy a special centerpiece, invite some friends over, and have a dinner party.

☐ *184.* Wear rose-colored glasses all
day. Buy an inexpensive pair of tinted
glasses to remind you to see everything in a
positive light today. Ignore all ugliness,
rudeness, harsh words, road hogs, bad news,
and everything political. You can get back to
reality tomorrow.

☐ *185.* Visit the home country (or
countries) of your ancestors. Before your
trip, find out as much as you can about
them. Then travel to their region, village,
city, or neighborhood. Perhaps you can even
find the street address of where they lived.
Visit churches of your ancestors' denomination, and ask to look at their old records to
see if you can find your family name.

☐ *186.* Visit the Statue of Liberty.
In October 1886, the statue (which stands
305 feet 1 inch high, from the ground to
the tip of her torch) was a gift to the American people from the citizens of France.
Since then, Lady Liberty has symbolized
freedom, hope, and opportunity to millions
of people. Until September 11, 2001,
visitors could ascend a spiral staircase up to
the crown, which offered a spectacular view
of New York Harbor. Legislation has been
proposed to reopen the statue's crown and
interior, but until that happens, visitors can
only enter the pedestal, which contains a
glass ceiling to view the framework of
the interior.

☐ ***187.*** Salute the troops and let them know how much you appreciate them for risking their lives to protect you and your freedom! Contact a USO office to find out how you can send a letter, card, or small gift as a token of your gratitude.

☐ ***188.*** Ride a bicycle built for two. Delight your companion as you sing:

"Daisy, Daisy, give me your answer, do.
I'm half crazy all for the love of you.
It won't be a stylish marriage—
I can't afford a carriage,
But you'll look sweet upon the seat
Of a bicycle built for two."
　　　　　　　　—"Daisy Bell" by Harry Dacre

☐ *189.* Step outside and close your eyes for 60 seconds. Identify as many sounds, smells, and sensations as you can. Then appreciate your sense of sight and behold all the beauty God has created in the world. Take a few moments to say a prayer of thanksgiving and repeat the prayer before you go to sleep.

☐ *190.* Learn to identify several constellations in the night sky. Many bookstores sell star maps, planispheres, and other tools to help you pick out your favorite constellations. Aim to learn every constellation in the zodiac. Before you know it, you'll be an accomplished stargazer pointing out constellations to others.

☐ *191.* Write a note thanking your parents for giving you life and for raising you. Write about specific things they did that taught you how to live your life. Share your favorite memories of family times. Detail your first childhood memory. If your parents are deceased, you will enjoy your trip down memory lane, and your children will treasure the letter someday.

☐ *192.* Go boating. You don't have to compete in a regatta to enjoy the benefits of sailing. Whether you're on a yacht, a pontoon, or an old rowboat, just get out on the water, and let the gentle sway of the waves relax you. Don't forget to wear a life jacket and to observe local boating laws.

☐ *193.* When an ice-cream truck comes around, treat the children who do not have any money to the flavor of their choice. Offer to buy them an ice cream every week if they perform a simple weekly chore for you or an infirm or elderly neighbor, such as bringing the newspaper to the front door.

☐ *194.* Stand under a waterfall. Feel the water rush over you as you experience nature's outdoor shower. Imagine that it's cleansing your soul of every insult, rejection, and unkind word you have ever experienced. Ask God for forgiveness and believe that the water is washing you clean of your pain and regrets.

☐ *195.* Drive across the country and absorb America's picturesque landscape. Drive Route 66 from Chicago to California, if you're so inclined. Although the original Route 66 was officially decommissioned in 1985, several interstate highways have portions dedicated as part of Historic Route 66. You'll be delighted by the intriguing billboards and kitschy attractions along the way, such as the Jack Rabbit Trading Post and the Cadillac Ranch. You can even spend the night in a wigwam at the Wigwam Village Motel. For step-by-step directions on how to meander this historic highway, visit www.historic66.com.

☐ **196.** Give an elderly neighbor a helping hand by mowing their lawn, weeding their garden, or trimming their hedges. If their fence needs painting, ask if you and some friends can paint it. Make a party out of it and be sure to include the owner of the freshly painted fence.

☐ **197.** Go snorkeling in the ocean. Get below the surface and view the dynamic sea life up close. Sea turtles, starfish, octopuses, rays, jellyfish, mollusks, minnows, bluefish, flounder, and vibrantly colored coral are just waiting for you to admire them. Take a disposable, underwater camera so the spectacular colors will never fade from your memory.

☐ **198.** Defy gravity by skydiving, bungee jumping, or diving off a cliff. If these are too strenuous for you, imagine you are a feather floating on a breeze, a marshmallow floating on hot chocolate, a toy boat bobbing in a pond, or sea foam on top of a Pacific wave.

☐ **199.** Stay up all night talking to a special friend. Share stories of childhood and school. Talk about your first love and your last. Explore your dreams and aspirations. Speculate on the future. Discuss topics of mutual interest. Tell at least one secret. Tell jokes and plan a prank. Be sure to have snacks and beverages available for the late-night munchies.

☐ **200.** Know yourself. As on a road trip, how can you get to where you're going if you don't know where you are? The same is true in life. How can you get to heaven if you don't know who you are or where you're going on your earthly journey? Just as you make an effort to know your friends, get to know who you are as well.

☐ **201.** Be thankful for your child's smile and all the experiences that give him or her something to smile about—the things you do, the things others do, the happy days and peaceful nights, the nutritious food you are able to provide, and the freedom you give him or her to play, pretend, and just be a kid.

☐ *202.* Watch a space shuttle launch. Check out NASA's Web site for a schedule of upcoming launches, including the location and details of the mission. Take a child with you and explain how recent space travel is. If you can remember the day humans landed on the moon, describe the excitement to your young friend.

☐ *203.* Buy a new car. Late summer is one of the best times to buy because dealers are trying to make room for next year's models. Perhaps you can't afford your dream car, but try to buy your favorite model within your price range. Take pride in owning your vehicle and enjoy that new car smell!

☐ *204.* Make a pilgrimage to a place
that inspires you. Perhaps it's a natural
wonder such as the Grand Canyon, Niagara
Falls, or Kentucky's Mammoth Cave. Maybe
it's a place where a person you admire lived,
such as Abraham Lincoln's childhood home
or Thomas Jefferson's Monticello.

☐ *205.* Make a date to do something
special by yourself and for yourself. Put a
note on your calendar so you don't schedule
anything else for that day. Treat yourself
like your own best friend, and respect the
time you spend alone. And don't be a cheap
date. Allow yourself to spend about the
same amount of money you would spend on
a day out with a friend.

☐ **206.** Sleep under the stars. Think about how infinite the universe is. Praise God for giving us a sky so vast we cannot even imagine where it begins or ends. If you see a falling star, imagine it's an angel on the way to answer a prayer.

☐ **207.** Adopt or foster a child. According to the U.S. Department of Health and Human Services, more than 250,000 children enter foster care each year. Worldwide there are thousands— perhaps millions—of children longing for a home and family life just like yours. Contact a reputable adoption agency or your state's Department of Children and Family Services today to find out more.

□ **208.** Swim in an ocean. If you can't swim, wade in just above your ankles, then walk along the shoreline. Take in the view and realize how vast the ocean is. Listen to the sound of the waves and the cries of seagulls.

□ **209.** Take a child berry picking. Be sure to wear long sleeves and pants to avoid mosquito bites, scratches, and poison ivy. Discuss all the different ways to use the berries you pick—in a pie or other special dessert, as an ice-cream topping, or with pancakes. Then, eat the berries the way the child chooses—even if it means you have pancakes for dinner or pie for breakfast.

☐ *210.* Try an exotic food—either cook it yourself or order something unusual at an ethnic restaurant. You may be the only person you know who ate an entire serving of tripe, okra, or rose-hip yogurt soup. And while you're in such an adventurous culinary mood, order or prepare an exotic drink or flavored coffee.

☐ *211.* Take a trip to the Grand Canyon, Washington, D.C., Yellowstone, Mount Rushmore, or some other great natural or historical site. Be encouraged by the positive and beautiful things the nation has to offer. Notice the care the government takes to keep these sites accessible to all citizens and visitors.

☐ *212.* Make a list of all the things
that are unique about you—your body,
adventures, joys, regrets, and sorrows.
Thank God for making only one of you in
the past and future history of the world. You
are one-of-a-kind in God's eyes. Feel the
love and acceptance of being his creation.

☐ *213.* Be the friend you want to
have. Be compassionate, not critical; be
thoughtful and on time; go with your
friends to a place they want to go. Pick up
the check and let them leave the tip. Ask
them to choose conversation topics and
look interested, even if you're not. Offer
them sincere compliments. Everyone has at
least one admirable trait.

☐ *214.* Witness a solar eclipse. But remember, don't ever look directly at the sun—it could cause permanent eye damage. Learn how to make a pinhole projector through which you can safely view a solar eclipse. Check online for annual schedules of both solar and lunar eclipses.

☐ *215.* Eat dessert before dinner, or just have dessert for dinner. If you get hungry later, you can always have a midnight snack. Try salad for breakfast and pancakes for lunch. Eat when you're hungry instead of at standard meal times. Try this for one day and see if you want to make small changes to your normal eating habits. There is no law against it!

☐ *216.* Host a foreign exchange student. Each year, American families host thousands of exchange students from countries all over the world. Contact your local high school to find out if you meet their requirements for host families. Talk to other host families to learn about their experiences. This mutually enriching cultural experience may bring unexpected challenges, but it also offers joys and a lifetime of memories.

☐ *217.* Go for a moonlight swim. Float on your back and meditate under the moon and the stars. Splash around like a child, then swim like an Olympic contender until you're tired.

☐ *218.* Ride a Ferris wheel with someone special. Celebrate the moment it stops at the top by telling your friend how special he or she is while you're on top of the world enjoying the best view in town. Ask your friend to pick another Ferris wheel for you both to ride next week, next month, or next year. Or just ride the same one together again.

☐ *219.* Jump off the high dive into a swimming pool . . . as long as you can swim, of course! If you don't know how to swim, now is a good time to learn. Progressing from wading in the shallow end to mastering a standard dive into the deep end is a great achievement that you'll be proud of.

☐ **220.** Watch a meteor shower. You can see random shooting stars at any time of the year, but a meteor shower is an entirely different spectacle. It's a gallery of shooting stars, and several occur each year. The most popular is the Perseid, which can be seen flying across the night sky from late July to mid-August. Your local meteorologist will usually let you know when to watch. It's truly a sight to behold.

☐ **221.** Watch a movie at a drive-in theater. There aren't many drive-ins operating these days; so if you have one in your area, take advantage of it. There's something special and nostalgic about seeing a movie on the big screen under the stars.

☐ **222.** Walk barefoot in the sand. Drag your big toe to make long, lazy curves behind you. Watch the waves fill your footprints. Step in sea foam and admire your lacy socks. Watch sand crabs scuttle into holes. Collect seashells and keep the most fascinating ones as reminders of a day when you had nothing better to do than walk in the sand.

☐ **223.** Ride in a limousine. Treat your friends and family or share the costs. Go to a nice restaurant, the theater, a party, or pack a picnic and have the driver let you off at a park. If you can afford only a one-way ride, take public transportation home or have a friend pick you up.

☐ **224.** Treat yourself to a bouquet of flowers. Display them at home or at work in a place where you'll see them often. Let the flowers remind you how creative God is to make so many beautiful colors, designs, and scents and how generous he is to give them to us for our enjoyment.

☐ **225.** Laugh at yourself. Being able to laugh at your mistakes is a sign of humility and grace. It shows that you don't take yourself too seriously and have a sense of humor.

"Laugh and the world laughs with you."
—from "Solitude" by Ella Wheeler Wilcox

☐ **226.** Attend a movie premiere. According to the Hollywood Chamber of Commerce, the best way to do this is to contact various movie studios and find out when they will be holding premieres and how to obtain tickets. Dress like a star and have a friend drop you off as close to the red carpet as possible.

☐ **227.** Take the scenic route. In the hustle and bustle of today's world, we're often in a hurry to get to our destination as quickly as possible. But once in a while, we need to slow our pace and take the road less traveled. It may take longer, but slowing down—on the road and in life—relieves stress and makes time for daydreaming.

☐ **228.** If you have not found your soul mate, start looking. This person has been in your heart all your life. Find a quiet place and think about where this person might be today. When an image arises in your mind, go to that place or plan a trip to that place. Be open to the possibilities and remember that what you are seeking is also seeking you.

☐ **229.** Go to a playground and release your inner child, the part of you that still wants to giggle, laugh, and play. Swing, slide, skip, and spin—just be a kid and have some fun. Remember, the Bible says that if you want to get into heaven, you must be a child at heart.

☐ **230.** Dye your hair. Try a totally new color that washes out after a few shampoos in case you don't like it. See if the new color makes you feel differently. Remember, God and your friends and family love you for who you are inside, not the color of your hair. And they'll love your spirit of adventure even if they don't like your new look.

☐ **231.** Volunteer in a struggling country. Instead of relaxing and getting pampered on vacation, give your time and energy to those less fortunate. Help build homes with Habitat for Humanity. Volunteer in an orphanage. Assist the Red Cross in a relief effort. If you can't make the trip, find out how you can help from home.

☐ **232.** Attend your class reunion. Whether it's your high school, college, or grammar school reunion celebrating 5 years, 20 years, or 50 years, reconnect with old friends and compare where life has taken you since you last met. Even if you didn't enjoy those years, you may be pleasantly surprised to learn how much (or how little) your former classmates have changed through the years.

☐ **233.** Be adventurous and go white-water rafting. You'll get drenched, but you'll also have the ride of your life, see some spectacular scenery, and experience a thrill that you'll remember for years to come.

☐ **234.** Send someone a greeting card for no reason. Remember how excited you were as a kid to get something in the mail? As adults, we dread getting the mail because it's generally bills, advertisements, and surveys that we just throw away. You can brighten someone's day by sending them a card just because.

☐ **235.** Stop and explore a landmark near you that you've never visited. Learn as much about it as you can. Your local library and historical society are good resources. Ask elderly people who live nearby about it. You may learn more than recorded history! If so, be sure to record it. Your local news-paper might be interested in publishing it.

☐ *236.* Take a friend's kids to the zoo for the day and give Mom a day to herself; double the fun—and double the blessing—if she's a single mom. Help the kids select a souvenir for Mom, and be sure they return home with a special memento of the day along with good memories.

☐ *237.* Go through an old photo album containing pictures of yourself. Remember the good times, the bad times, the proud days, the scary days. Acknowledge to God that he has been with you every day of your life. Thank God for never leaving your side, even at the hardest times. Also, thank him for sharing your pride and happiness during the good times.

☐ **238.** Climb a tree. Use a ladder if you need to, but find a safe perch somewhere off the ground. Take a book if you want or a stack of memories to relive. Stay in the tree as long as you can and enjoy a bird's-eye view of the world.

☐ **239.** Practice courteous driving. Remember, you're not the only one on this planet, and the streets were not built just for you. Welcome fellow road warriors with a cheerful bumper sticker. Share the road, let other drivers cut in from time to time, and above all, don't tailgate or make ugly faces at other drivers no matter how rude they may be. You can set a good example instead of compounding a problem.

☐ **240.** Today, dedicate your life to the Lord. Pray, "Jesus, I am yours. Help me to understand my purpose here on Earth. Guide me to the path you have written my name on, and help me to be the person I was created to be. I love you." Do this as often as you wish. It may become a habit!

☐ **241.** Write a letter now to your future children or grandchildren. Describe for them what life was like before they were born. Let them know how much you are looking forward to meeting them. Express your wishes and dreams for their future and the kind of world you hope they grow up in. Give them one piece of advice, the most important thing you have learned in life.

☐ *242.* Buy a copy of your favorite story from childhood. Read it to a child and tell them what you liked about the book when you were their age. Personalize the book by writing their name and yours, along with the date, on the title page.

☐ *243.* Take a walk in the woods—specifically a redwood forest, if possible. When you trek among the giant sequoia trees of northern California, you'll be reminded of the strength and enormity of God's love. These are the tallest trees in the world, often measuring more than 350 feet high. They can also live to be 2,000 years old; some sprouted during the Roman empire and have survived far longer.

☐ *244.* Grab a pair of binoculars and examine the full moon. (A telescope is better, but binoculars offer a satisfactory view.) Look at the ripples, ridges, and craters. Also, learn which planets are visible, and try to spot them.

☐ *245.* Who do you idolize? Determine what you admire about that person and work on developing and nurturing those traits in yourself. If you can talk to the person, ask them how they developed their skills and other good qualities. If your idol is a celebrity or historical figure, read their biography or autobiography. With research and hard work, you can become like the person you admire.

☐ **246.** What is your signature song? "Born to Be Wild"? "Dancin' Queen"? "Amazing Grace"? Determine your signature song, learn every stanza and every verse, then sing it at karaoke—singing every word and trying to hit every note on key. You should probably practice in the shower first.

☐ **247.** Laugh so hard that tears run down your cheeks. You know what it takes to get there: a TV show, a book, a silly thing that your friend does, a phone call to a friend who shares your sense of humor, that e-mail joke you've been saving because it's too good to erase. Push your own funny button. You know where it is.

☐ *248.* Return the tools you borrowed from your neighbor. Make sure they're cleaned, sharpened, and stored in proper containers. Discuss what you accomplished with them. If they're gardening tools, take something from your garden as a thank-you, even if it's just a few tomatoes or a small bouquet of flowers.

☐ *249.* Determine one or two things that you're really passionate about. It could be a charitable cause, a sport, or a hobby. Find out how you can get more involved with those activities, then take action!

"We must be the change we wish to see in the world."

—Mahatma Gandhi

☐ **250.** Reconnect with an old friend. Seek or offer forgiveness if you parted in anger. Talk about the good times you shared and plan ways to spend time together again. Devote time and energy into keeping the friendship alive. It is all too easy to let the busyness of life sweep friendships into a neglected corner.

☐ **251.** Get an education. Whether you go back to school to get your high school diploma or GED or get a college degree or a doctorate, knowledge is one of the greatest gifts you can give to yourself and to the world. Use your new knowledge to understand other people and cultures, politics, and to educate your children.

☐ **252.** Write a letter to somebody who has inspired you. It could be someone you know, a celebrity, or somebody you've admired from afar. Whether you admire their work, their physical abilities, or their kindness and generosity, let them know how they've inspired you, motivated you, and had an impact on your life. They'll appreciate your kind words.

☐ **253.** Go camping. Relax while you take a break from technology and the stresses of everyday life. Leave the portable DVD player, iPod, and video games at home. Turn off the cell phone and use it only in case of emergency. Explore the wilderness and get in touch with nature.

☐ **254.** Sign up to be a bone marrow donor. Every year, more than 35,000 people in the United States need bone marrow transplants to save their lives. Visit www.marrow.org or www.abmdr.org to find out more and check your medical eligibility online. It may be inconvenient and you may experience some pain, but you'll be saving a life, so it will be worth the sacrifice.

☐ **255.** Write down ten things that make you smile. Post them on the refrigerator or on your wall at work and review them when you need a pick-me-up. Thank God for them as well. And then ask God to help you find ten more things to smile about. Watch the list grow longer as the days pass.

☐ **256.** Let go of grudges and offer forgiveness. Holding on to a grudge affects you more negatively than it does the person with whom you're upset. Left to stew, the bitterness of a grudge affects your mood, your energy level, your outlook on life, even your health. Remember, Jesus took the punishment for the sins of all humankind. Let go and let God handle the offense.

☐ **257.** Make someone's day. Do one thing today that will mean a lot to someone. A phone call, an e-mail, or a hug mean a great deal to someone who is hurting. A bouquet of wildflowers and a card are tangible signs of your friendship. Share a piece of cake and share a memory.

☐ **258.** Make an anonymous donation. Large or small, give what you can
afford to the first need you come across.
Keep it between you, God, and the angels.
Know that when you're in need, there is
truth in the phrase, "What goes around
comes around." Keep the cycle of good
karma and compassion in motion.

☐ **259.** With a child or group of
children (adults are welcome, too) play a
game you used to love, such as hide-and-
seek, hopscotch, tag, or jump rope. Allow
yourself to feel like a kid again. Remember
why you used to love playing and why it was
so hard to leave your friends when it was
time to go home.

☐ **260.** Break a world record. Check out the Guinness World Records Web site to find out how you can make a record attempt. Everyone should have at least one claim to fame. Find out where you have the greatest potential to do what no one else has done or to do it longer or in the most unusual place.

☐ **261.** Scream from the top of a mountain. There's nothing quite as liberating as climbing to the top of a mountain, then shouting for joy at your accomplishment and listening to your echoes. A mountaintop is one of the best places in the world to release pent-up emotions. You'll feel much lighter in spirit on the walk down.

☐ **262.** Fall helplessly and hopelessly head over heels in love. Considering all the variables that need to come into play to make this happen—such as the timing and the chemistry—if you find one true love, hold on to that person for life. Remember that relationships need to be nurtured and that sometimes you will have to compromise and make sacrifices.

☐ **263.** Write a screenplay about one of the most memorable events of your life—or a story you've heard about your ancestors. It can be as short as one act or as long as you are inspired to write. Select the best actors for each role, and sketch the stage settings.

☐ *264.* Visit at least one of the Seven Wonders of the Natural World—the handiwork of God himself: Mount Everest, the Grand Canyon, the Paricutin volcano in Mexico, Victoria Falls in Africa, the giant sequoia trees in California, the Northern Lights, and the Great Barrier Reef in Australia.

☐ *265.* Babysit your grandchildren, nieces and nephews, or children of a close friend to give the parents an opportunity to spend time alone together, renewing their friendship and love. If possible, plan to spend the night so the parents can stay out as late as they want. The kids will enjoy the slumber party!

☐ **266.** Memorize a favorite poem. It can be a nursery rhyme to share with young friends or a sonnet to recite to a lover. It can be a limerick that makes you laugh or a ballad with many verses to pass the time spent in grocery lines and traffic jams.

☐ **267.** Cross the international date line, an imaginary line in the Pacific Ocean at the 180° line of longitude. It makes several turns around various countries to prevent any territory from being divided into two separate days. By traveling west across the international date line, you will gain or repeat a day; by traveling east across it, you will lose or skip a day.

☐ **268.** Learn a foreign language. The world as we know it is getting smaller and smaller. Not physically, but in today's world of globalization, the ability to speak a foreign language is an invaluable skill.

☐ **269.** Recipe for Joy:
- Fear God and trust him
- Keep a running conversation with him
- Be thankful
- Forgive others and do not judge
- Confess and repent from your sin
- Listen to God and do what he asks you
- Read his love letter, the Bible
- Love others

Mix well and take a portion every day.

☐ *270.* Learn to drive a stick-shift
(manual transmission) automobile. You
never know when you might have to take
over the wheel if a driver becomes incapacitated. Rental cars with automatic transmission cost more to rent in Europe—sometimes twice as much. For both safety and
financial reasons, the ability to drive a stick
shift is an important skill to master.

☐ *271.* Visit Niagara Falls...in both
the United States and Canada. Take photos
of both views and select your favorite to
have enlarged and framed. Have a picnic as
close to the Falls as you can comfortably sit.
Buy a souvenir from each country as a
memento of your visit.

□ **272.** See an endangered species in its natural habitat. Did you know there are more than a thousand endangered species in the world? For a list of endangered and threatened species, visit the Web site of the U.S. Fish & Wildlife Service. Find out what you can do to help so that future generations will be able to enjoy these animals.

□ **273.** Meet your favorite celebrity. Their schedule may be posted on their Web site. If the situation is appropriate, ask for an autograph. But don't bother them while they're eating dinner or enjoying a family moment. Remember, celebrities are people, too. They like to keep their fans happy, but they also need some time to themselves.

☐ **274.** Set a realistic goal and push yourself until you achieve it. Write your goal in your planner, tape it to your bedroom mirror, carry it in your pocket, and slip it into your Bible. With God's help and blessing, you CAN make it happen!

☐ **275.** October is Fire Safety Month. Test your smoke alarm and carbon monoxide detector today and on the first day of every month. Teach fire safety to everyone in your household, and make them aware of escape routes from every room. Then, hold a surprise fire drill. Visit the Web site of the U.S. Fire Administration for safety tips, and be sure to check out their kids section.

☐ *276.* Let go of the past. Holding on to old hurts, regrets, grudges, resentments, and unattainable dreams will only cause you pain and keep you from moving forward. Realize that yesterday is in the past; it's over; you can't go back and change it. Look ahead to the future. But live for today, one day at a time.

"For yesterday is but a dream and tomorrow is only a vision. But today well lived makes every yesterday a dream of happiness and tomorrow a vision of hope."
        —Kalidasa, 1st century Sanskrit poet

☐ **277.** Initiate a conversation with the person sitting next to you on a long flight (if the person indicates a willingness to talk). You just might make a lifelong friend. But if the person sticks his or her nose in a book before takeoff or takes out a stack of paperwork, you should assume conversation would be unwelcome.

☐ **278.** Witness the Changing of the Guard at Buckingham Palace. During this shift change, the new guards march in to replace the old, keeping in step with the tune of the Guard's Band. The crowd will contain people from all over the world. Listen and see how many different languages you can identify.

☐ *279.* Know someone in the hospital? Offer to babysit, pack lunches, do laundry, help the kids with their homework—the list is endless, so base it on something that you do well and feel comfortable doing. And make sure it is a needed service. Your hospitalized friend may have three people doing their laundry but no one to help with homework.

☐ *280.* Find your hidden talent. Maybe you've always been extremely gifted. Most of us are not so fortunate. Even if you think you're not at all talented, everyone has a special gift. You just need to figure out what it is, then hone it until you've reached a level of skill that you can be proud of.

☐ *281.* Take off your shoes, roll up your pants, and stomp grapes in Tuscany. If you can't get to Italy, find a closer vineyard. Many wineries host grape-stomping competitions during their annual grape festival. You can learn how grapes go from the vine to bottles of wine and be a part of the process as well.

☐ *282.* Practice random acts of kindness. Everywhere you go today, look around and see who needs what and what needs doing. Help someone with packages board a bus, pick up litter, visit a shut-in, share your umbrella with somebody who doesn't have one, feed a stray animal. Check out www.helpothers.org for more ideas.

☐ *283.* Help end world poverty. We live in a world of surplus. With the resources and technology we have, thousands of people should not die every day from a mosquito bite, or from lack of food, clean water, or proper medical care. Yet in Africa and other parts of the developing world, that is the reality. To find out how you can help end extreme poverty, visit www.one.org.

☐ *284.* Hold a chimpanzee. If you've ever dreamed of cuddling up with a friendly chimp, do some research online to find out where and how you can do this. Discover the traits you have in common with one of these furry creatures, and see how well you can communicate with your new friend.

☐ **285.** Ride a mechanical bull. It's not as easy as some people make it look, so go slow and don't be a show-off. Most mechanical bulls have various levels of difficulty, so take it easy and don't start at the highest level no matter how hard your friends press you. (Do not attempt if you're pregnant or have back or neck problems.)

☐ **286.** Finish a marathon . . . or go as far as you can with the intent to finish. Of course, this requires discipline and extensive training, but you'll be surprised at what you'll learn about yourself and what your body is capable of in the process. Then, start looking for your next challenge and push yourself even further.

☐ **287.** Participate in an organized (nonviolent) protest for something you strongly believe in. You can sit back and complain about an issue, but nothing will change until people get together and make their voices heard. Be part of the solution, not part of the unhappy, inactive majority.

☐ **288.** Experience weightlessness. So you wanted to travel into outer space but a career as an astronaut just wasn't in the cards? Now you can experience the thrill of floating and flying through the cabin of a special zero-gravity parabolic airplane. These special flights are available in Fort Lauderdale, Florida, and cost around $3,000 for a day-long excursion.

□ **289.** Witness the birth of a child. Comfort and encourage the mother and cut the umbilical cord. There's nothing as awe-inspiring and life-affirming as watching a new baby coming into the world. The overwhelming feeling of God's love and power through the miracle of life is truly a life-changing experience.

□ **290.** Visit Mecca. Mecca (also called Makkah) is located in Saudi Arabia and is considered the holiest city of Islam. A pilgrimage to Mecca, known as the hajj, is one of the Five Pillars of the Muslim faith. Millions of Muslims attend the hajj each year to pay homage and feel closer to God.

☐ **291.** Travel around the world. You can get an around-the-world ticket from an airline, or you can use various modes of transportation from a mail boat to a rickshaw. Depending on your level of courage, you can travel without buying tickets in advance. Just arrive somewhere, look around, decide where to go next, and hop aboard the first vehicle going that way.

☐ **292.** Write a note to your political representative or send a letter to the editor praising a person or group that is doing good things in your community. Complaints always outweigh praises, and a person who is doing good may be wondering if he or she is making an impact.

☐ **293.** Spend one day where everything you pray to God is an offering of thanks or praise. It's not difficult to find things to be thankful for when you decide that it's your mission for the day. You'll be surprised how important the small things you encounter every day can become.

☐ **294.** Watch the Chicago Cubs win the World Series! Although the "Men in Blue" haven't been World Champs since 1908, they have a national following of fans that support them win or lose. When the Cubbies finally make it to the World Series, you can be sure that the whole world will be watching and waiting to see if the curse has finally been broken.

☐ *295.* Give a favorite relative a phone call today. Tell them they were the person you thought of when you read this suggestion and explain why they popped into your mind. Share a few memories of times you spent together, and ask about their first memory of you. If feasible, make plans to get together.

☐ *296.* Stay in a five-star hotel. Go all out and order room service. Enjoy the hotel's amenities including the hot tub, sauna, pool, beauty salon, and the candy on your pillow. Ask the concierge to get you tickets to a play or a local sporting event or attraction, and have the doorman hail a taxi for you. Don't forget to tip!

☐ **297.** Be a movie or TV show extra. Besides just showing up on a movie or TV show set and trying to get noticed, the best way to become an extra is by registering with a casting company. This typically requires a nominal fee of about $25. Also, do some research online for tips on how to avoid scams.

☐ **298.** See a penguin in its natural habitat. There are several places to view these special creatures up close and per-sonal, all of which are in the southern hemisphere. Some of the places you can visit penguins in their natural habitat include New Zealand, Australia, Argentina, and South Africa.

155

☐ *299.* Host a dinner party. Many entertaining books and Web sites offer tips, menu suggestions, and ideas on how to incorporate a theme such as a Hawaiian luau or a murder mystery dinner party. Use place cards and put some thought behind where to seat people. Recruit your children or young relatives or neighbors to serve the meal and clean up afterward.

☐ *300.* Smile and make eye contact with every person who serves you today— waitstaff, cashiers, newspaper delivery person, etc. Be sure to thank each one and ask their name. The next time you meet them, greet them by name. The world will seem like a friendlier place to both of you.

☐ *301.* Attend or host a costume
party. You used to love to play dress-up as a
kid, so why not now? When you dress in a
costume, you can be anything or anyone you
want to be. If you're timid, you can be bold.
If you're the life of the party, you can be a
wallflower. A costume can loosen your
inhibitions and set your spirit free!

☐ *302.* Instead of Halloween candy,
give trick-or-treaters pre-read or gently
used children's books. These can be purchased for as little as ten cents at garage
sales and library book sales. Friends and
neighbors may give you their old books for
free. Dress in costume and be willing to
read short passages to your young visitors.

☐ *303.* Spend the night in a haunted house. Visit www.hauntedhouses.com to find a spooky site near you. Take snacks and a good book because you may not be able to sleep. Take a camera and a tape recorder to document a potential supernatural visit. Call the local newspaper if you have a ghostly experience.

☐ *304.* Write a song or poem for a loved one. There's nothing more meaning-ful than a personal expression of love and devotion that comes straight from the heart. It doesn't have to rhyme and you don't need to use fancy language. Write the way you talk, and your thoughts will come naturally and sound natural as well.

☐ *305.* Change churches for one Sunday. Try a different denomination and keep an open mind and an open heart. During the service, look for things that are similar, not different from your church. Remember that living "outside the box" expands your horizons and keeps you open to meeting new people. Besides, there will be no denominations in heaven.

☐ *306.* Perform on stage. Join a community theater, sing karaoke, participate in an open-mic night, or sing in the church choir. Performance anxiety or stage fright is a real issue for many people, but once you overcome it, embrace your chance to shine in the spotlight.

☐ *307.* Get out and enjoy the beauty
of autumn leaves changing colors. Better
yet, invite a friend to spend a day on a fall
foliage road trip. Pack a picnic and a good
map. Meander, don't rush through the forest
paths and do not preplan your picnic spot.
When you get hungry, the perfect place will
be right around the next bend.

☐ *308.* Feed the birds. Scatter bread
crumbs on your lawn, or purchase a bird
feeder and some bird food and hang the
feeder outside. Then watch the birds eat the
meal you provided for them and be thankful
for the many ways God provides for you.
Don't be surprised if you attract some
squirrels, too.

☐ *309.* Return to your hometown
with your family. Take them to your former
school and places you liked to hang out.
Tell them stories about your childhood and
show them where they unfolded. Help them
get to know you better by understanding
what life was like growing up there.

☐ *310.* Write your will. You may
dread even the thought of this because it
means facing your own mortality. But as a
legal document, a will ensures that your
loved ones understand your final wishes and
that they will be carried out. You will spare
your loved ones from making difficult and
uncomfortable decisions. Contact your
attorney to get started.

☐ *311.* Come clean about something you've been hiding—a lie, a fear, an old hurt, or a grudge that you need to let go. Confess to God first; receive his forgiveness. Then, determine if there's anyone else to whom you need to confess. Pray for courage and wisdom, and then confess your secret. Sometimes a letter is better because it gives the receiver time to think about your confession before responding.

☐ *312.* Make your own clothing. You don't have to be the next Vera Wang or Tommy Hilfiger; just one simple item will do. Take a sewing or knitting class if you need to, then wear your handmade item with pride.

☐ *313.* Pursue a dream. Your dreams and desires shape who you are. And what you do about them says a lot about your personality. Do what you can to make them come true before it's too late.

"Don't start living tomorrow; tomorrow never arrives. Start working on your dreams and ambitions today."

—Anonymous

☐ *314.* If you see a person or a pet lost and in distress, stop and help. Remember whatever we do for "one of the least of these" (the most vulnerable and helpless among us), we do for Christ. It's not just a nice idea, it's an order from our Creator.

☐ *315.* Connect with an animal. If you've ever owned a pet, you know that God put them on Earth to keep humans company. Scientific studies prove that owning a pet reduces blood pressure. But being a pet owner is a big responsibility. So if you're not ready for such a commitment, consider pet-sitting for a friend or volunteering at an animal shelter or horse ranch. Ask a local veterinarian where you can volunteer.

☐ *316.* Be thankful for the kindness of strangers. Remember times when you needed help, and—like an angel—a helpful person appeared. Think about the goodness of ordinary people who get no press coverage because, typically, good news is no news.

☐ *317.* Color with a child. Unless you overanalyze your color scheme or worry too much about going outside the lines, coloring can be a relaxing and fun activity for adults as well as children. While you're coloring, talk to the child about their life's ambitions. Tell them what yours were when you were their age.

☐ *318.* Live in a foreign country. There's no better way to immerse yourself in a foreign culture than to live there. You'll learn to speak the language (hopefully), eat the cuisine, see the historical sites and monuments, and view the world from an entirely different perspective. And you might even make some lifelong friends.

☐ *319.* Visit the Vietnam Memorial Wall in Washington, D.C. Of the three monuments to the Vietnam War in the nation's capital, "The Wall" is clearly the most recognizable. It makes no political statement as it simply, yet respectfully, lists the names of more than 58,000 soldiers who lost their lives during the war or are missing in action.

☐ *320.* Next time you see an active-duty military person or a veteran, stop to thank him or her for serving to protect your freedom. If appropriate, ask them about their time in the service. Some war stories are hard to hear, but maybe the person you ask needs to talk about it.

☐ *321.* Frame a special picture that makes you smile every time you look at it. Display it where you'll see it often and let it fill you with joy, peace, and love when you remember its significance.

☐ *322.* Teach a child to cook. Most young children welcome the opportunity to learn a few mysteries of the kitchen. It doesn't have to be a gourmet dish, but helping to make a meal fills a child with feelings of independence and responsibility. It makes them feel grown up. However, it should be made clear to the child that they should not attempt to cook anything without an adult's supervision.

□ *323.* What do you love to do?
What are you good at? What makes you
laugh and smile and forget all your worries?
What do you do that makes others laugh or
feel special or pampered? Do one or two of
these things today, and thank God for
creating you with these unique talents.

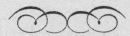

□ *324.* Write down some of your
most loved verses of scripture, and hide
them in your coat pockets, cupboards, and
glove box. You'll be planting seeds of
encouragement to surprise yourself in the
future. You may find a particular verse on
the day you need it the most. Or someone
else may find it when they need some
uplifting words.

☐ *325.* Start a new family tradition, such as serving a special food on a particular holiday, visiting a favorite restaurant on a special day, or writing your own prayer of grace to say before family meals. Whatever you choose, make it unique to your family and use it often.

☐ *326.* Learn something new. Take a class or join a group to learn something that interests you. Pursue it with passion until you master it to your satisfaction and can teach it to others. If you're stuck for ideas, try the alphabet idea generator: A is for Arabic, B is for bookbinding, C is for candle making. . . . Your personal alphabet will reveal your interests.

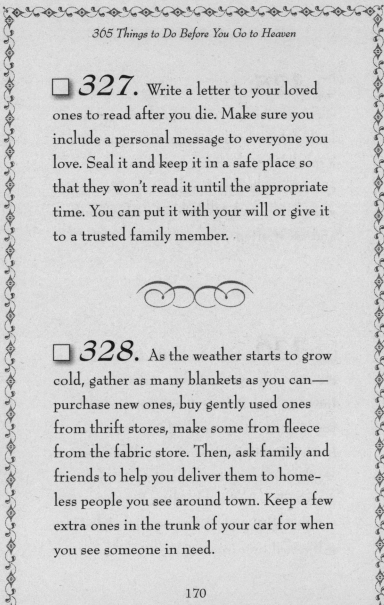

☐ **327.** Write a letter to your loved ones to read after you die. Make sure you include a personal message to everyone you love. Seal it and keep it in a safe place so that they won't read it until the appropriate time. You can put it with your will or give it to a trusted family member.

☐ **328.** As the weather starts to grow cold, gather as many blankets as you can— purchase new ones, buy gently used ones from thrift stores, make some from fleece from the fabric store. Then, ask family and friends to help you deliver them to home- less people you see around town. Keep a few extra ones in the trunk of your car for when you see someone in need.

☐ *329.* Swallow your pride. Many times the hardest thing to do is say "I'm sorry" or admit that you were wrong. But humility is rewarding. It lifts big burdens from your shoulders and frees your spirit. Your confession will lighten, and maybe relieve, the heart of the other person as well.

☐ *330.* Rock a baby to sleep in a comfortable chair. Breathe in the scent of baby powder and lotion. Stroke the baby's tender skin. Hold its hand and look at each tiny finger and toe one by one. Sing your favorite lullaby and rock until the baby falls asleep. If you have time, rock the baby until it wakes. Remember that this day will not come again, not for you or the child.

☐ *331.* Have something published, whether it's a major novel, a simple poem in a magazine, or a letter to the editor. You know what you want to write. Don't let fear get in the way. Just sit down, start writing, and don't worry about the spelling. No one else will read it until you're ready to make it public, so just be sure to proofread it before you submit it.

☐ *332.* Pay the toll for the car behind you. Pump gas for the car behind you at the gas station. Let the car behind you have the parking space you are first in line to claim. Let the person behind you at the grocery store go ahead of you. Remember that Jesus says, "The first shall be last."

☐ **333.** Be thankful for:
- family and friends
- health
- employment
- home
- safety
- food and water
- clean clothing
- transportation

Then, take this list and make it personal. Name the family members you are thankful for, describe your good health, list your friends and favorite foods. Wear your favorite piece of clothing even if it's a swimsuit and it's snowing outside. (We recommend you wear something over it, though.)

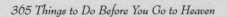

☐ **334.** Be a hero or inspiration to somebody. Be worthy of somebody's admiration. Determine your best trait and exercise it as often as you can. Admit your worst trait and commit to improving it little by little, day by day.

☐ **335.** Offer to help an elderly neighbor, friend, or relative decorate their house for the holidays. They may have treasured Christmas decorations that they have not been able to display for years because they require ladders and physical agility. Ask them about their holiday memories and spend some time with them. Don't forget to take the decorations down after the holidays are over.

☐ **336.** Get in touch with your artistic side. Take up pottery or learn to paint, draw, sculpt, weave, or write. Don't worry if your first attempts look like grade school projects. Expertise comes only with lots of practice. What if Michelangelo had given up when he saw his first attempt to make something beautiful from marble?

☐ **337.** Make up your own recipe for holiday cookies, candy, or eggnog and then give it a name. Package your masterpiece in festive tins or bottles and give away as gifts to neighbors, teachers, hosts at holiday parties, and friends at work. Make up several extra packages for local retirement homes. Include a card with the recipe.

☐ **338.** Start planning a three-generation villa vacation for next summer. The Lucca area of Tuscany in Italy has something fun and interesting for all ages. If you rent a villa, you will have a home to return to after a day of soaking up the sun at the beach or art and culture in quaint little villages. Besides, it costs less than a hotel. Research online to find the perfect villa for your family.

☐ **339.** Before your feet hit the floor in the morning, open your Bible and read a psalm. Begin your day with praise and worship. Think about the psalm during the day and how it relates to what's going on in your life. Read the psalm again at bedtime.

☐ *340.* Decorate a box with a slot in the top. Label it "Wish Box" and place it in a prominent place in your house. Set a pencil and a pad of paper next to the box and encourage family members and visitors to write down a wish and put it in the box. Before Christmas, read all the wishes and try to make as many come true as you can.

☐ *341.* Learn to practice faith. Whenever you are confronted with a problem, go to God first in prayer before trying your own solutions or asking others for advice. God may lead you to the person who has the answer, or you may find the answer in the song of a bird, a certain slant of the sun's rays, or in your own heart.

☐ *342.* Look through art books until you find a painting or sculpture that strikes you as beautiful or mysterious. See the original if possible. If not, get a print and hang it on the wall. Think about why this work of art strikes you so deeply. You may learn something about yourself that only art can reveal.

☐ *343.* Give up the best parking spot or seat on the bus to an elderly person, remembering that we should put others before ourselves. If you have to walk farther or stand longer, start praying instead of complaining to yourself. Be grateful that you were able to give this little gift today to someone who did not expect it.

☐ **344.** Attend a performance of your favorite band. Allow yourself the freedom to lose yourself in the music. Jump up and down, dance, and sway to the beat. Don't worry about making a fool of yourself. Your friends won't mind and who cares what other people think!

☐ **345.** Be a Secret Santa. Contact your church or local elementary school to find out which children could benefit from a Secret Santa. Obtain a list of their wants and needs, then deliver the gifts to their home. You can even dress as Mr. (or Mrs.) Claus if you like. Or take the child shopping to purchase gifts for his or her family members as well as himself or herself.

☐ *346.* Extend grace and mercy. Say a prayer or bless someone who doesn't deserve it, such as a rude salesclerk, the person who cuts you off in traffic or steals your parking spot, or a friend who is treating you unfairly. Choose to do so with a loving spirit and expect nothing from them in return. Believe your blessing makes a difference, even if you cannot see it.

☐ *347.* Choose a charity to support, but find out how much of your donation will go to actual services. You probably don't want to help pay for a charity's corporate jet, so check their Web site or call and ask what percentage of your donation will go directly to program services.

☐ *348.* Adopt a needy family at
Christmas. Find out their sizes, likes, and
dislikes. Then purchase gifts such as clothing, as well as toys for children, CDs, books,
DVDs, and beauty products for adults.
Supply a full Christmas dinner and a tree.
Consider making it a group effort with your
coworkers or friends, or cut back on your
own family's Christmas budget—it will be
well worth it.

☐ *349.* Take a warm bubble bath by
candlelight. Play some relaxing music,
drink champagne, read poetry, and eat
chocolates. Let all the stresses of the day
melt away.

☐ *350.* Help people help themselves.
Learn about micro-credit and how a
$20 loan will help a woman in Asia or
Africa start a small business that will feed
her children. Prepare to be amazed because
98 percent of micro-credit borrowers pay
back their loans—and these are some of the
poorest people on Earth. For more information see www.microcreditsummit.org.

☐ *351.* Kiss an elderly person under
the mistletoe and whisper in their ear how
special they are to you and to others. Tell
them how glad you are to see them, and
wish them a happy Christmas and a year of
blessings. Then do the same with the young-
est person in the room, even if it's a baby.

☐ *352.* If you witness an accident, stop and offer assistance (towels, blankets, cell phone usage, water bottles, a statement to the police). Do not move injured persons, but offer to pray for those involved. Stay until the police and paramedics have stabilized the injured, and offer to drive uninjured family members or passengers home or to the hospital.

☐ *353.* Be a Christmas angel. Leave a small wrapped gift under the Christmas tree at church for a child who is not popular with the others. Check with their Sunday School teacher about appropriate items. Do not sign your name. Make this a Christmas tradition for the same child each year.

☐ **354.** Gather a group of people to sing Christmas carols door-to-door in your neighborhood, at a hospital, nursing home, or retirement center. If in a public place, such as a hospital, always get permission from the activities director before you arrive and ask how long you can stay. The patients or residents will also appreciate cookies and other holiday goodies.

☐ **355.** Let someone cut in line. During the hectic holiday season, it seems everyone is in a hurry. So if you have the time and you see somebody who has only one item, is struggling with impatient children, or seems to be in a bigger hurry than you are, let them go ahead of you.

☐ **356.** See the world through the eyes of a child. Watch a child experience the joy of Christmas and let it remind you of your childhood holidays. If you don't have young children of your own, you can watch children visit Santa at shopping malls and watch them skip home on the last school day before the holidays.

☐ **357.** Sing carols with family and friends at a Christmas gathering. Bring song sheets for everyone so you can sing all the verses. Afterward, ask each caroler their favorite holiday song and why it is special to them. Your question may unlock a beautiful memory or a heartwarming story. Be prepared to tell the first story to break the ice.

☐ **358.** Go to a candlelight Christmas Eve service with family or friends. Go alone if necessary. Cherish the beauty of Christ's birth represented in the nativity scene, the special Christmas decorations, and the symbols throughout the church. Let the music fill you with joy, and honor the Prince of Peace by thinking about how you can be a peacemaker.

☐ **359.** Look through old photos with your family and Christmas guests. Recall the good times of Christmases past, and retell old stories. See if anyone has a Christmas story they have not yet told. Remember those already in heaven. Share memories of them and tell their stories, too.

□ **360.** Make a list of at least
25 things for which you are grateful today.
Write a love letter or thank-you note to
God. Be specific about why you are grateful
for everything on your list. See how many
items are answered prayers. If you think
about it, you may find an answer to a long-
ago prayer you had forgotten about.

□ **361.** Go to the top of the Empire
State Building in New York City. From its
completion in 1931, it reigned as the
world's tallest building until 1972, when it
was outdone by the World Trade Center and
then the Sears Tower. At the Observatory
on the 86th floor, you can take in a pan-
oramic view of the grand New York skyline.

☐ *362.* Imagine yourself a year from now. What can you change today to make next year better? Write down the things you need to do in the next year to make yourself the person you want to be. Put your list in a place where you'll see it every day, and be reminded of the person you want to become.

☐ *363.* Attend a Broadway show. With nearly 40 theaters on Broadway, there are plays and musicals to suit almost everyone's taste. And buying tickets is not as difficult or as expensive as you might think. Day-of-show tickets can often be purchased at half price online.

☐ **364.** Live with no regrets. Make peace with your life. If there's something you've been longing to do . . . do it. If you're unable to do so, accept that it wasn't part of God's plan for you. Let go of any lingering disappointment, and move on. Be open to discovering God's special plan for you; you may not be able to see it until you let go of an impossible dream.

☐ **365.** See "the ball" drop in Times Square on New Year's Eve. Share the moment with family or friends. As you ring in the New Year, know that people around the world are joining you in song and spirit. Make a toast to a new year filled with peace, happiness, and a multitude of blessings.

Places I Want to Travel to
Before I Go to Heaven

_____

_____

_____

_____

Adventures I Want to Experience
Before I Go to Heaven

_____

_____

_____

_____

_____